8:15 MY DARKEST HOUR

8:15 MY DARKEST HOUR

BRENDA CAMPBELL

8:15 My Darkest Hour

Copyright © 2019 by Brenda Campbell. All rights reserved.

No part of this publication may be reproduced, stored in a retrieval system or transmitted in any way by any means, electronic, mechanical, photocopy, recording or otherwise without the prior permission of the author except as provided by USA copyright law.

The opinions expressed by the author are not necessarily those of URLink Print and Media.

1603 Capitol Ave., Suite 310 Cheyenne, Wyoming USA 82001
1-888-980-6523 | admin@urlinkpublishing.com

URLink Print and Media is committed to excellence in the publishing industry.

Book design copyright © 2019 by URLink Print and Media. All rights reserved.

Published in the United States of America

ISBN 978-1-64367-394-3 (Paperback)
ISBN 978-1-64367-393-6 (Digital)

26.04.19

8:15 MY DARKEST HOUR

BRENDA CAMPBELL

8:15 My Darkest Hour

Copyright © 2019 by Brenda Campbell. All rights reserved.

No part of this publication may be reproduced, stored in a retrieval system or transmitted in any way by any means, electronic, mechanical, photocopy, recording or otherwise without the prior permission of the author except as provided by USA copyright law.

The opinions expressed by the author are not necessarily those of URLink Print and Media.

1603 Capitol Ave., Suite 310 Cheyenne, Wyoming USA 82001
1-888-980-6523 | admin@urlinkpublishing.com

URLink Print and Media is committed to excellence in the publishing industry.

Book design copyright © 2019 by URLink Print and Media. All rights reserved.

Published in the United States of America

ISBN 978-1-64367-394-3 (Paperback)
ISBN 978-1-64367-393-6 (Digital)

26.04.19

My name is Jane. I was born and raised in the small town of Gladewater Texas born to parents late Earnestine Green and the late Billy Hanson. We are six siblings in the family, three boys, and three girls–Christopher, Billy, Glory, Joseph, Rebeckey and my late brother Lonzie. I'm the eldest of them all.

When I was younger, my family and I lived in a small town called Gladewater Texas. Things were good and bad in the early years of my life. As the years went on, I never expected to be shocked, sad, and happy.

Many things have happened to me in my life, and this story is the worst and saddest thing. This story is about me and how I've struggled and overcome all my obstacles and developed into a very strong woman. Writing about my darkest hour is the hardest thing in my life, the hardest and most disturbing, yet it is also interesting. As I sit here and reevaluate my life, I now know where to start.

One of the lessons I have learned is how certain things have happened in my life and how they have made me a better and stronger person. All the things I've had to fight in my life have kept me moving forward and have helped me hold my head up higher and higher—all the fears and pains that I've found in myself and the journeys I've been on.

I've found myself fighting battles that I cannot win, fears and pains that have been difficult for me. Everything in my life is ending, just like a light that has gone out of my head, and I can never get it back. I've never thought I can ever get that light back again for all my life as I continue writing through the rough times. As described in **Matthew 27:27–46**, *the darkest hours for Jesus Christ are from the sixth hour until the ninth hour. Jesus cried, "My God, why have you forsaken me?"* The hour that Jesus was left alone in anguish, a time when no earthly man could come to his aid to deliver him or comfort him, a time when even heaven itself must have turned a deaf ear to his cry, caused Christ himself to cry out loud in acknowledgment that even his Father had abandoned him.

When we are reminded of the price that our master has paid for our sins, we are much more impressed with the passage that reminds us of the price of redemption.

God has gotten me through so many rough times. God has saved me so many times in my darkest hour I completely lost count. God is telling me and reminding me that he is always a shining light to my life, and the whole time, he has been preparing me for my journey. He lets me know that he is the light shining through my darkest hour. In those hours, in the storm that I went through as a mother, which I thought I could never come out of, God was right there amid everything, through all the pain, troubles, grief, and death that I had to face. It was terribly hard for me.

In **Psalms 18:28**, *God lights our paths when we are walking in darkness.* I will feel the heavenly flames. It's time to trust my God and rest upon his name.

This story that I'm telling is about my only son. As I lead you through this tough journey, I must go through it heartbroken. It is about a child that was stripped of his life; he never got the chance to experience his own life.

The day I gave birth to my son Cadarrius Green and throughout my pregnancy, I used to say things to him. As I carried him in my womb, I talked to him. I sang to him. I told Cadarrius, my love, the fears, and the promises that were held for us the day after his birth. I knew I had been given a bundle of joy.

Cadarrius was nine pounds and ten ounces. He was just a very cute baby, and as the years went by, Cadarrius developed into a very handsome young man, until that day, that horrible evening, when every mother's nightmare happened: getting a phone call and having everyone tell you that your child had an accident.

That day was March 16, 2010. I was at work, just getting off at about 2:30 p.m. I got home, took a bath, sat down to relax, and watched TV for until about eight thirty. I was so tired and sleepy I decided to go ahead and go on to bed. I just got comfortable and went on to sleep well. A couple of hours later, I had a disturbing phone call. My daughter called me, and in the past, she had always told jokes. She said, "Mother, Cadarrius had been in an accident! He just got his foot cut off!"

I told her to quit playing and that I was tired. I hung up the phone, and it had not been minutes later when my nephew called and said, "Jane, it's true! Cadarrius did get his foot cut off." He was jumping over the train, and his pants got caught under the rail of the wheel of the train.

The train had started moving slowly, and he could not do anything while the train was moving. It started dragging him, my son, under the train and my nephew. It was not going fast at that moment, but it was starting to pick up. Some of the force of the train pulled him under it.

My nephew, Rodrick, risked his life and got under there. Some of my son's toes had popped out, and his foot had melted to the train rail. Rodrick had to pull him; he was stuck to the train. While it was still dragging, some of his other body parts were becoming dismembered. Rodrick pulled him from the train while his leg was in the middle of the track. They finally rushed him to the hospital with one pint of blood left after the train had finally gone through.

My daughter; Korneshia, his sister, picked up his leg and foot and ran all the way to the hospital, crying and discombobulated. She handed her brother's foot and leg, and the nurse took and threw them into a bucket. She didn't put it on ice or anything.

He had been in the emergency room for thirty minutes, and my son was still sitting there. The nurse was still calling other patients into the room. My son was in worse shape, and he was still just sitting there.

8:15 MY DARKEST HOUR

Finally, they took him to the back. He was all delusional, out of his head. He didn't know who gave him morphine, and I thought they were going to airlift him to American Hospital. But they drove him by ambulance.

When he got there, the team was already on standby, waiting for him. I called the doctor and told him I was coming, 'cause I was so shaken up to be in the ambulance. My daughter was there with him. The trauma team told me they were going to do everything they could to save everything.

Well, after that, I was just speechless as the doctor started treating his third-degree burns. They tried to attach his foot back. They couldn't. Instead, they had to cut his leg, and they just kept on cutting until they cut all the way above the knee.

This brought my son back in the room a couple of days later, after the infection had been drained out of his leg. It was showing up, and he got an infection and had blood clots. After that, the doctors rushed him back to the emergency room, opening the wound.

He was crying and in pain and asking where his foot and leg were. My son was just screaming and hollering, saying he wanted his foot and his leg. I tried to comfort him, but he was so angry and mad he was not trying to hear anything I was trying to say. He was so frustrated and just out of his mind for about thirty minutes.

After I calmed him down, after I got him, I just played him on my lap, and I rubbed his head and back and said that he was going to be okay. And I told him that he wouldn't get his physical leg back; he would have to get a replacement.

His response was, "I don't want a replacement.

I want my leg and foot back."

I told him, "Listen, my child. Whenever you leave this old world, your leg and foot will be there waiting for you, so don't worry."

And from that day on, I never mentioned another word about his foot and leg.

The nightmare that I had to go through along with my son was a life experience for both of us. I know now that everything was for a reason and was just a season in the plan that God had in his hand. God had his hand on us the whole time, and with the power of God, it didn't seem like he was not there; the whole time, he was there.

In **Romans 8:25**, *God said, "If we hope for that we see not, then we do with patience wait for it."* As I see life in the mountains of triumph and valleys of impatience, I have discovered, as a mother, a few things about the valleys. I recognize the valley is always waiting for me; the valley waits for the answers to our prayers. And as I look, the valleys are always looking back and reviewing. The Lord himself remembers all the tough times.

I know now that everything in my life has happened for a reason. Sometimes I ask myself why. Why am I going through this? I just didn't understand, but now I know God is making me stronger. I must march on with a task to complete.

When I told my son the day, he lost his limb that I would move heaven and earth if it were possible, I meant it from the bottom my heart.

The day my son lost his leg and his foot put a strain on me, and it was very stressful for me when my son turned seventeen years old. It was sad for me just looking at the pain on his face. I just couldn't imagine that this was all in favor of God.

He stepped in and said, "I'm going to send your son an advocate, a counselor, an encourager, a helper, and a persuader to get him through all these—all the suffering, all the pain." God had stepped in and said, "I have found all these people in you, his mother."

When the day he was released from the hospital came, I still held his hand and rubbed his body when he was still in pain. I was my child's crutch when he was too weak to walk to prepare his meals. That was when the healing process began.

This message I'm giving should be lived each day. Take each day as a gift, enjoy a joyful laugh each day, and add the appreciation for every moment you have on earth today. Tomorrow is not promised to us. Today you may be here, and tomorrow you may be gone. I have to sit back and give thanks for each day that I see the sunrise because no one can predict when it will be the end of my time. Between life and death, this is the time to give all the praises and thanks.

8:15 MY DARKEST HOUR

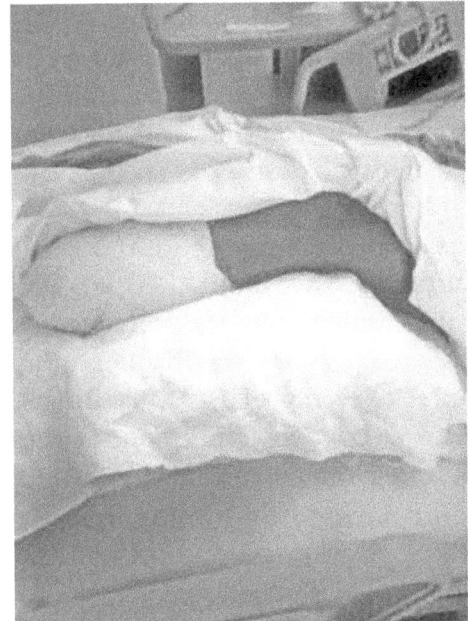

In this next story, I'm going to talk about how I woke up thinking about how and what I should fix for breakfast, thinking about what time I should pick up my child from school, but the last thing I expected as I prepared him for bed was that I was always planning for him and then he would not be there anymore. This next story is so horrible I just cannot believe I'm still here.

My job as a mother was to protect my child and raise him the right way. Then suddenly, this child died, and at that moment, it was like my brain was not functioning correctly anymore. As a mother, my heart was broken, and it was like a veil had dropped over my eyes. Everything I saw was black. I had raised my son, my only son, to the age of seventeen years old, and I raised him and watched him as he grew, matured, and started blossoming into his own life.

It was very devastating when I lost my child and lost the future, I could give to a teenager who never got the chance to experience life. His life was cut short.

The message that I'm giving is very powerful, and I just hope I can help others who have already been or are going through the same situation. This message I have as a mother is a relation a child has between the two, God and Satan.

As I go on to speak, if you train your child in the right way, that child will not leave. From my experience in this situation, when a teen is left alone in this world, he is controlled by two powers—the good and the bad, the right and the wrong, God and Satan. Everyone in this world has been challenged by these two forces. All of us in life must choose which way we like to live and the path we want to take.

This unexpected death of my son just tore my world apart. This was the darkest hour I would have never dreamed of. I had always been startled by late-night phone calls. I had always feared hearing something bad, and I always prepared myself for the worst and the unexpected. But this call I received took all the strength from my body, my soul. It was like someone had hit me so hard in the stomach, like a pain I could not get rid of.

I started breathing so hard, and I got so dizzy when I got this tragic news. My child Cadarrius, my sweet, kind, and loving child that God had sent me from above. He let him be with me a little while before he called him back home.

This life-changing experience had dramatically been an awful tragedy for all the wrong reasons. This tragedy had to happen to me. I found the unthinkable could happen. It was very tough for me the day I got this unexpected call.

Another lesson I've had to go through is that all parents who have children who have experienced car accidents and have very serious injuries are left scarred for life, heartbroken, bitter, sad, and confused.

As parents, as mothers, we must go through a lot, especially when we are single parents, with all the emotions of going through losing a child in a car wreck. As I've experienced, the emotions one goes through in losing a child in a car wreck, the fear of that person not being in your life or on this earth anymore, are a hard thing.

Now as I look at it, there are no safe teen drivers. Their inexperience can lead to fatal errors. Every day now, when I cut the tune or listen to the radio or even listen to all the news reports about teen drivers, it saddens me and my heart to know that I am listening about all the teens in the world who have been killed or have died in car crashes caused by a driver that over speeds.

Every year, there are teens dying in car crashes or in fatal accidents before or after graduation. But in many states, a lot of parents help their children get access to the most dangerous thing in the world, and that's the keys to parents' vehicle. That's the most dangerous thing in the world for a teen driver, yet a lot of parents move the little thing out of a child's way, so he may not get harmed.

You see parents who, when the baby is just learning how to walk, push tables out of the way and wrap the tables' corners. Now that's learning how to walk. Then you may see mothers who get their children their first bicycle that has training wheels when they're just learning how to ride, and later, the same children start to ride without the little wheels. All is good, and all that's basic training.

At home, parents are already preparing their children how to drive a vehicle, so by the time the children reach the age of fifteen or sixteen, after they have developed, what the parents do then take them out to get their permits and licenses. The worst thing you can do is let them get their permit to drive.

The parents that put the keys in their children's hands are the same ones that sit back, cross their legs, cross their hands, and then pray to God that their child will come back home in one piece. But what about the ones that don't come back home and are taken to the funeral home instead? While other parents are giving this little story, I'm writing about an introduction to a car wreck in talking about myself.

My son was seventeen years old. My son didn't have the chance to explore the world. He lost his foot and leg, and he lost his life in a fatal car accident. In telling this story, I hope I can continue without tears, knowing that my son, Cadarrius, seventeen years old, had been killed in a fatal car accident.

Cadarrius was the last in the family. He was the baby boy, my only son, the last one to graduate, and he didn't get to make it. Cadarrius had four sisters, who loved him dearly. They all had a good bond, like the one I had with him. If anyone knew him very much, that would be his sisters, cousins, and all his friends.

Cadarrius was a very kind, caring, compassionate, loving, and kindhearted young man. My son was a blessing from God above. My son had a personality that was genuine. He drew crowds of people around, him. He had one of the smiles you could not resist.

My son was here on earth for a purpose. On the day my son Cadarrius was stripped from this world in the blink of an eye, I didn't know what the next second, minute, or hour would bring to him or the family. My son had already planned thing he shouldn't have. All the plans he had planned in that very second were gone also in a second. He was gone in a second.

It all started out after my son lost his leg. His departure from the hospital was a very good process. After months from the hospital, he started having therapy. Cadarrius started throwing huge parties every weekend, and they were the biggest parties you could have imagined. People from everywhere were coming out of town, flying down to his parties.

But this was the day his life ended.

Everyone was getting ready for the New Year party. But before they went outside and started a bonfire, with everyone around, his sister came out of the house to check on him to make sure he was okay. And out of nowhere, he pulled his sister to the side and asked her if she saw all those dead people reaching for him. It shocked my daughter. She ran in the house and called and told me.

I was speechless; my heart was like jumping out of my body. I then looked up to heaven and said, "Lord, I know warning comes before destruction."

By that time, everyone was getting everything together. This party was the talk of the town. Everyone knew except me. That night, I visited my son and his sisters and told them that I was going home to get some rest. I had just left Dallas, Texas. My grandson had surgery, and I and my husband were tired. So, we left then.

Cadarrius had everything going, good for him. He loved his life. Until the night I received an awful phone call. It was very disturbing. That call was death. It came to my door, knocked, and then came back three days later. It came back and took my child. I knew, that night, death swooped in and got my son like a thief in the night, like a wind just blowing through, and it never returned. In the blink of an eye, it took his soul and left the body on December 30, 2010, at about 8:15 p.m.

My daughter rushed into my bedroom, holding the cell phone with fear, terror, and confusion, insisting I take the phone call. I picked up my cell phone to see what time it was. My daughter knew she had no business coming into my room this time of night. I had a twelve-hour shift planned for the next day.

"Hello," I answered, tired and disoriented.

It was my youngest daughter. "Jane, Cadarriusis dead."

"What?" I answered. I yelled out, very alert at that time, "No, he's not!" I denied it, very unsure of my reply.

I had my daughter's phone to my ear, but while I was holding my phone, I couldn't help but realize I had fifteen missed calls.

I hung up in my daughter's face and immediately got out of bed to call my son. I called, and he answered. "Hello."

"Cadarrius!" I yelled out.

"You have reached my voicemail. Leave me your number."

"No, this cannot be happening!"

Why haven't I shed any tears yet? Is this really happening? What should I do next? I had a million things running through my head.

My phone just kept ringing off the hook. I didn't want to talk to anyone, so my husband took the phone from me and said, "I will talk to everyone. You just stay calm."

I couldn't stay calm for anything. I was frantic, just pacing the house while my brain was in shock. My brain still could not register, and I could not get it to register that my child was dead.

At eight thirty, I was out the door with the keys in my hand. I don't know what I did after I got up. I was so discombobulated I don't even remember brushing my teeth. My mind was on my child.

My husband stood in front of me and told me to give him the keys and that I was not going to drive. We didn't have time to argue about it. I got on the other side of the car and sat with tons of thoughts in my head of what had happened. The way I thought it happened was not how it happened. I just thought it was a misunderstanding. I thought it was nothing major, and I kept the good thoughts in my head and kicked the negative ones out.

My husband finally put the keys in the ignition and backed out and gone ahead to drive forward on this forty-five-minute drive to Gilmer, to my second home.

It had not even been three minutes into the drive when I asked my husband, "Can you drive any faster? Oh, I wish I could fly over all this traffic! These stoplights are too long. Why is the radio on?" I snapped at my husband. "My son's dead, and you want to listen to the radio? Get me to my son!"

He knew I was shocked, so he didn't rush on; he just went about ten miles per hour. *Why is he driving so slowly?* We were going seventy- five miles per hour in a forty-five-miles-per-hour zone.

I called my daughter back. "How did he die?" I asked.

She answered, "A car wreck?"

I hung up in her face. I cried out to God, "Please, Lord, let my son be okay. Please, Lord. I'll go to church every Sunday and Wednesday. I'll change, Lord. I'll be a better mother. Lord, please."

After that prayer, I was confident that the Lord had heard me, and I was sure that my son was okay.

At nine twenty-three, I pulled into the town of Summerfield. My daughter said he died on the road. We took the time to get to the house soon as we approached Highway 49. My husband and I stopped for a second, and he asked me if I was okay. I told him yes. "Whatever you see, just know you're not alone."

But I was alone. He was only his stepfather.

He didn't feel how I felt.

He tried to speed down the street, and I asked him to slow down. There were cones everywhere, caution signs, flares, parked cars, and his car parts were there.

"Stop the car!" I yelled. "Stop the car now! Why is it an *x* is sprayed right there, painted in red? Right there in the ditch." I had such a bad feeling in the bottom of my stomach. Something was not right.

I remembered the prayer I had with God. "Hassock," I told myself, "I got to keep my faith strong. I can't doubt now."

My husband and I got back into the car and drove ten minutes down the road. At ten, I pulled up to my house. It was so strange that there were over ten cars parked in front of the house. I opened the door, and I was approached by about twenty grieving high school students and Cadarrius's algebra teacher and science teacher.

"I'm sorry for your loss," everyone emotionally told me one by one, some together. "Where is my son?"

One of his classmates said, "On Facebook, it says he's already at the funeral home."

"What funeral home?"

"funeral home," someone answered. "Here's the number."

We all sat in silence for what seemed like twenty minutes. I kept hearing Cadarrius' voicemail coming from several phones in the area.

"Oh my god, I forgot to tell my other daughter what is going on. She is the fixer. She can fix this," I told my husband.

He just sat in silence, looking at me with tears in his eyes, knowing that my son was really dead.

I didn't want to accept it.

"Excuse me, everyone." I pardoned myself outside to call my daughter. It just rang and rang. I went back into the house and told my husband we had to go to Diana to tell my other daughter.

He replied, "What about the guests?"

I just excused myself again, and I let them know I needed to get to my other daughter and that they were welcome to stay at home until I got back. Everyone was like a family to me.

Anyway, my husband thanked everyone for coming to support us and our family, and he accompanied me to my other daughter.

At about eleven, I knocked on the front door. My daughter came to the door, and I told her, "You know I would not just show up at your home unexpected, but there has been an accident."

She replied, "What kind of accident?"

I said, "It has something to do with your brother."

She said, "Is he all right?"

I said, "No. He was in a car wreck." Tears were streaming down my face. "No, he has been killed."

She ran and grabbed her cell phone and tried calling her brother. Frantic and nervous, she called her husband. He was out of town. She told him that her brother had died. He rushed back. My son and his son-in-law were very close. My daughter was still pacing. I was also pacing, thinking about my son and her brother. I was praying to God, still asking God what to do from that point on. I picked up my Bible and started reading **Matthew 11:28:** *"Come unto me, all ye that labor and are heavy laden, and I will give you rest."* And in **Psalm 18:28**, I read,

> *"The Lord will enlighten my darkness."*

Well, the next day, we had to be at the funeral home at 11:00 a.m. We got to the funeral home, went in, and talked to the director and took care of the paperwork. And then I asked if I could see my son, and the director said, "He is not going to look like he was when he was on earth, so be prepared."

The funeral director rolled my son in there while we were in the lobby, and we pulled the sheet from his head. He had glass all over his head, and I could see that he was ejected from the car and thrown into a ditch. He had hit his head on a pipe, which pierced through his skull. He had bruises all over his body. He was just completely messed up. As a mother looking at her child, I was just speechless. I looked at my son on that cold table, and he had a smile on his face like he didn't have to go through any pain or suffering again. But now, as a mother, I must go through the pain and suffering for the rest of my life. I must deal with not seeing or hearing him talk, with not having him say "Good morning" or "Good night," bring my coffee or even give me my flowers. He used to always tell me, "I'm going to give you your flowers while you are still here Mom because when you leave this world, you won't need any, because you cannot smell them."

I just sat in the funeral home, and those words came to me. I couldn't do anything but just break down and cry and ask why my son had to leave this world. I really didn't have much time with him. I loved my son so much. I just didn't know if I could survive something like this.

The director went back and said, "We have to take him back in there. I'm so sorry."

I didn't want them to take him back in there. I just wanted to get him up and say, "Come on, Cadarrius. It's okay. Mother is here to take care of you."

As I cried, my knees just buckled, and my husband had to catch me. I just kept saying, "Please don't take him. Please don't take him." I just felt like someone was touching me. My soul felt like it just wanted to go out of my body, so I could be free with my son. That was how bad I felt looking at him, knowing that I would never see him physically on earth anymore.

At this point, I was clueless. I didn't know what to do. I wanted to shut down, and I didn't want this time to be around anyone. And I hadn't even buried my son yet. My mind was running everywhere. I had lots of questions, and I didn't know if I ever wanted to talk again. I didn't know. Now that my son was gone, my joy, my laughter, my heart…I just didn't know what and how to expect the departure of my child.

8:15 MY DARKEST HOUR

The day of January 5, 2011, everyone was getting ready for the last day to see Cadarrius. Everyone met up at home and went ahead to drive to the church. When everyone was in the church, it was crowded inside and outside. I was the last one to go in.

Once the director and my husband walked me in the church, I felt ice-cold. Everyone in the church just stared at me. You could have heard a pin drop. It was so silent. As I got to my seat, I couldn't do anything but stare at the casket. He was just like a baby. He left from this world as my baby. Just like when he first came into this world and I wrapped him in a blue blanket when he left out of this world, I wrapped him again in a blue blanket, but the disturbing thing that got me was that I had no support. None of my children were behind me, nor were my brothers or sisters, and that hurt me more. But I couldn't think about that while burying my child on that day, even though my feelings were hurt twice.

Soon as we left the church to go to the grave site, the director said some words. I started watching them lower my child into the grave. As a mother standing beside the grave that was dug for her child, I just wanted to fall in there with him. My head was hurting me so bad it was like everything was spinning. As they lowered his body to the ground, I was looking and thinking he was all alone. I knew we come in this world all by ourselves, and I knew we have to leave here all by ourselves. I just wanted to tell them, "Don't put him under that cold ground. It's cold. I know his body is a body and that he doesn't know that blood is not running through his veins anymore."

As I talked to God, I said, "Ashes to ashes and dust to dust, I give him back into your loving arms. Not that your son is no longer my son physically. Your child is now back safe with you."

Everyone went ahead back to the church and ate. Finally, after everyone was done eating, everyone gave me his or her condolences and headed home.

As for me, this was when everything began. I just completely shut down. I stopped talking to everyone. My husband was so helpful. He really didn't know what to really do or what to say. I had no energy when I got back home. I was lying, looking at the ceiling, just waiting for God to come to get me. That was how bad I wanted to leave this world, going through all these withdrawings.

I had given up. I was very depressed. I stopped eating. I lost weight down to fifty pounds. My husband did everything to get me to eat and go outside. He did my baths and put me back in bed. I could hear him crying to God, asking him to make me better so I wouldn't be in this shape.

For two years, it was very hard and difficult being confined in the house.

My husband finally started getting me to put my clothes on and started taking me outside. He said, "I'm not going to let you fall off the face of the earth. I'm going to stand by you no matter how long it takes for you to get over your son's death."

I just partially cried.

8:15 MY DARKEST HOUR

One day, my children came over to the house, and I was back in bed again. My grandchildren, Arianna and Terrell ran into the room. They always knew that I always kept a smile on my face, and they saw me in the shape they thought I was going to die. I felt like that. That was why I wanted to lie in bed until God came for me, but when I saw my grandkids with tears in their eyes, I couldn't get any sadder.

I was already sad and depressed, and they went into the bathroom and got some towels and washed my face and said, "Granny, get up. We need you."

I just cried and cried when they told me this. I knew then it was time for me to get up and get my life back on track. I knew it was time for me to move on and get ready to start a new chapter in my life. I had to learn to get help, so I could get healed.

I knew this was a slow-moving healing process. I had to give myself time to grieve even though I had to get away from family and friends. I was not trying to rush the grieving process.

As days, weeks, and months went by, it was so hard. All the lonely nights. I couldn't get over the funeral; it was like a burning in my soul, like a deep gash, like a scar issued in my life that would never fade away. It was like a lightning had struck my brain, pieces just left everywhere. My memory was like nonexistent in my brain. It was like a virus to me. But that was my grief. I felt just like an old computer. My brain . . .

I just felt like all my child's records and files had been deleted. It was like I could no longer recall his record in my brain. They were all gone.

As I continued to stay shut up in my home, just walking and staring around the empty place, with no one to see, my tears just started flowing down my face again. I just remembered my child's smiles.

I knew one day my grief would cease and my tears would start drying up, but right that moment, I was at a crossroad, developing my grief process.

After all the weeks, days, and months of staying shut up and getting all these out of my system, I started feeling better and beautiful. For me, it was now a white scar rested on my skin, and then a brown one because of the sun, like an old gash that reminded clearly of the depression from my old wound that had closed and faded away.

It was because of this miserable problem in my life that I had now realized that I had to let it fade into the distance.

For my son, a young man, he had always given everyone a reason to get through another day. He loved everyone; he loved everyone in his own way. He had always wrapped his arms around everyone. He loved everyone to the fullest. He cared for everyone.

I sometimes used to sit by the window with the window up, and I would just listen to him talk to God to make everything right. The big smile he had with that bright, twinkling light he had in his eyes just made me cry every time I looked at him.

Now all my tears were sorrows. The tears that I had for my son were the job. I knew the love heaven was wrapped in was also wrapped around my son. With all the suffering that I had gone through, there was no explanation to me. All I felt was that I just wanted the suffering to end. All the suffering from losing my son, I just wanted it to go away. Just be gone.

I knew that in order for me to face the problem, I had to deal with the problem. I had to take charge of my life again. Through all the disappointments, I had to recognize the spiritual path that was causing the suffering. Everyone expected me to move fast or move on their own terms.

My suffering had devastated me. It was so hard for me to understand. I didn't think I would ever get an answer. Jesus suffered and died and then rose for us.

In **Isaiah 54:4–11**, *God says there is so much pain and hurt so many rejections, so much lioness.* In **2 Corinthians 1:3**, *the Word of God says that he is the Father of all mercies and the God of all comfort we know at one time or another.* I've found myself like David in the Bible, asking, *"How long, Lord?"* (**Ps. 13:1**).

We ask God to end the suffering we experience, but in my suffering, I didn't know what God was preparing for me. In **John 21:15**, it is said that *when God does use us, he encourages us to build his kingdom with vigor.* God is our rock and our shelter. I will never forget the pain and suffering Christ has gone through for us. No one has ever suffered more than our Father in heaven had. No one has paid the price dearly for all our sins. It was God who paid for our sins and was crucified. No one in this world has suffered more than our Father in heaven had. When Jesus stretched his arms out and died, he showed us how much he loved us. It is God himself who asks us to trust him when we are suffering, when our own loved one cries out in our presence.

For all the changes and suffering that happened to me, I had to look at our Christ and see what he had gone through.

As I keep reading, in **Genesis 50:20** it is said that *God turns suffering around for good.* In the Bible, Job suffered, and we see a man come into a deeper understanding with God. Then we see Joseph, someone who was able to say to those who hurt him, "What you meant for evil against me, God meant for the good of many." As I look at these people in the Bible with their suffering, I realize that God tests those he has chosen before he uses them mightily. As I live every day with the storms God has sent me, I need to know if I am strong enough to make it through the clouds. I have to learn each day how to deal with the storms that I've been through, to know each day God won't put any more on me that I cannot handle.

All I know now is God has just been preparing me for the storms. I know now that God has prepared me to go through the clouds. It has really made me a stronger and better person. I just really had no clue at that time what my duty was, but the whole time, God was using me. And I thank God for that every day, for this experience, for using me to get through something so I may be able to help someone else who's going through what I have been through, through the understanding that I have now.

The tragedy with my child was the death I had to battle. God gave me the choice to fight my battles myself or to just let my situation go and let him work it out in my favor, facing the battle and becoming one of his soldiers for him. God gave me enough time to start learning increasingly about him, to be able to walk with him and to learn more about the Bible. I just had to sit back and continue to control my life. God sat back to see how long I could take these storms and be ready to go through the clouds. God had already decided the length of time he had to work on my personality and my scarification.

I now know it was a process. God has gotten me through my deepest water. As I've read in **Psalm 39**, *the Lord says that to this day, tears will still flow down my face.* I know now that I cannot let go of God. I've learned the sun will rise with healing in its wings. Until it does, we may learn to be in a safe place to fall, cushioning the blow of suffering.

With all the storms that were placed in my life, I had to learn my purpose. What God was trying to tell me by preparing my life. I had to learn to deal with all the storms in my life day by day.

It's funny how the days go by so fast.

I was burying my son, and the following year, I ended up burying my husband. One day you are married, and then one year later, you're all alone, single again.

I know we all must leave one day, but I've never thought my husband would leave that early after raising my children and then getting adjusted to marriage. I didn't expect it. It was so difficult. I had become numb and depressed, was having anxiety attacks, and was isolated again. It was something I was trying to avoid. It was another death. I found myself in a place I didn't quite want to be, being alone again.

On November 27, 2011, my husband had a massive heart attack. We were at home, just got through eating, and I went into another room to do something. When I went back out, he was standing in front of me. I asked him if he could see the two fingers, and he said yes.

I said, "Okay, then."

The next thing I knew, he collapsed on the floor. I ran out of the kitchen, and he was on the floor. Blood was coming out of his mouth. I called 911 and told them I needed an ambulance at my home and that my husband had collapsed. The 911 operator asked me to check his pulse. I did it. I could hardly feel it. Then she asked me if he was breathing. I said, "Barely."

She said, "I need you to give him CPR and twenty chest compressions."

I told the operator my husband was bleeding in his mouth. I cleaned it and did what I was asked. The paramedic had gotten there, and they did everything over again and told me that his heart had busted and he was living off the defibrillator. So they rushed him to the hospital. I was crying, and one of the ambulance guys told his wife to take me to the emergency room until they were finished with my husband.

But I already knew he was gone.

Well, here came the doctor, and the nurse came in and took me down the hallway to another room. The doctor sat with me. I asked them if my husband was gone, and they said, "Yeah."

I said, "What am I going to do without my husband?"

I was very sad and was crying. Then someone asked me if they could make the calls for me, and I just took it easy.

The preacher came in and talked with me and everything. Then they called my husband's family and called my family to let them know what had happened.

Later on, someone from the hospital drove me back home. By that time, my children were there and wanted me to go back home with them. I wouldn't go, so they went back home the next day.

I went to the funeral home to make arrangements for my husband. I got everything taken care of. Then I had to turn around and take care of the funeral and didn't have any support. I had no one at the funeral but one cousin, one brother, the preacher, and the guys who dug the grave. Besides me, there were two guys who carried my husband's casket.

That's very sad and very disturbing to me, how I didn't have anyone there to comfort me. To me, death is a simple part of the cycle of life. I am still trying to alleviate the pain of losing my husband, and what I have in my heart and in my soul will never be whole again. Through all the storms I have been through, I thought I could not pass it. But God was working with me, keeping me on the right path, and that was good for me. I just thank God for working in my favor through two deaths. It was rough. It was a big rough patch in my life, especially when I didn't have any support from family and friends. But I made it without them.

I love my family. I used to have a family that was so involved. I grew up in a house that had thrown insults at me for years. I also felt a lot of jealousy toward me. My family used to always tell me, and until this day, that I'm not a part of the family. Their intention was to always hurt me. They did succeed and did a good job as I would be in so much pain and was scared, they would do something to hurt me. I had to look over my shoulder. For me now, it's like looking into a mirror of everything I've been through.

They've scandalized my name, told my friends that I was not supposed to be their friend. They told lies on me, and even my siblings turned on me. They treated my children very badly. Mad at them, they let my children get out of their beds when I had to work and made them sleep on the floor. They made them eat food they didn't like, made them smoke, beat them just to torture me, called cops to get my children taken away from me, made them drink large cups of water. When they wanted to eat, they gave them hot sauce and pepper.

When my children were twelve, seven, six, and four years old, they grabbed them by the neck and threw them on the couches, made them stand on corners until they fell down, locked them outside until I came in from work. Luckily, it was not cold.

One day, I was off from work and was in the kitchen, fixing my children something to eat. I had my back turned. Luckily, someone outside saw my sister come into the house. I had my back turned, so I didn't hear her come in. She had a bottle. Someone saw her; she was going to hit me on the head. The back door was open, so I ran out. My neighbor was out there, so she turned around and left before the police got there.

They called or came to my job and got me fired. Many times, I needed to go to the store, and everyone had cars and could drive, and I couldn't. At that time, I would ask them to take me to the store. Their response was "Walk."

Well, I did.

I had one daughter who couldn't walk, so I had to carry her on my shoulder because I couldn't get anyone to take me to the store. Even her father, who walked out on me, knew I needed help, but he just left me for another woman because he couldn't deal with our child. Well, I was so depressed, sad, lonely, and had no job—nothing—just all alone raising my children.

I never let anyone see me cry. I tried my best to keep a smile on my face. It was hard for those troubled times. It was a wonder that I didn't lose my mind, and I thanked God every day for keeping my mind. And I kept my mind on God the whole time. All the strength I had in my body was just drained. I felt like all the walls were closing and crashing down on me. It was like all my blood was leaking out. That was how tired I was.

But I couldn't give up. I had to keep going for my children's sake. God kept his angels and his arms around me the whole time. My siblings put me through hell all because they had a problem with me.

There's not a day that goes by that I don't think about what they had done to me. At that time, my family wounded my soul. I could never do anything to hurt them. All the people that I hung around or encountered, they would say bad things to them, and they would get a kick out of it. I just looked at them and said, "They really don't care about me, because if they do, they will not do or say the thing they've said and done."

No matter how good I was to them, my siblings still treated me badly. I would ask them, "What have I done for you to treat me the way you treat me?" They'd just look at me and laugh. I tried my hardest to be a good sister to them.

I didn't know how much I could take from them again. I had started getting tired, and one by one, I started letting them go. They had started to become a poison in my life. This was not the environment I wanted to be in.

As I read in my Bible, in **Ephesians 6:10–12**, it is said, *"Be strong in the Lord, and in the strength of his might. Put on the whole armor of God, that you will be able to stand against the schemes of the devil. For we do not wrestle against flesh and blood, but against the rulers, the authorities, the rulers of cosmic powers in this present darkness, against the spiritual forces of evil in the heavenly places."*

With all the ability I had, I could have hated them, but I didn't have hate, not a bone in my body. I disliked what they had done to me. I had to choose if I would want to love or hate. I asked myself, "What would Jesus do?" He would choose to forgive and pray and love.

In spite of everything my family has put me through, all kinds of hell, I have forgiven them,

and I've moved on with my life without them. I've learned that when you love your family, you put their name in a circle, not a heart because a family can break your heart. But when you draw a circle, you can always go on forever.

I remember an old saying that the old people used to say: "Life is too short to wake up in the morning with regrets. It is always best to love the people that treat you right." And I do believe that.

I learned to worship God in my daily life. I learned that before I could drive a car, I had to fill it up first, then I could start with my daily journey. On that road sign that I ran into were the obstacles in my way. The car had failed, and it had sent me to a dead end.

I learned that all the obstacles that were in my life had and did make me sick and nervous. And they had led me to a lot of anger, despair, stress, and depression. I've now realized that I was driving too fast, and I just knew that I was going the wrong direction. I now know that my life was like a park, so I just had to stop, and I had to park my car—meaning, I had to look at my life in a different way. I had to lay my head on the steering wheel, and I just had to call on Jesus and just say, "Lord, I don't know what to do anymore."

The obstacles didn't disappear, so when I started to pray more and started trusting more, God started guiding me in the right direction. I just had to sit and stop and just listen to God's voice, and I had to start regaining my insight.

I prayed for God to renew my mind, body, and soul. I asked God to show me a better road to life and where I needed to be.

An important experience in my life reminds me that before it ends, I have to hear the noise rush but never forget to live and learn.

I learned that I could not learn things backward, and I had to live moving forward. After facing all the hardships, I know God wanted me to trust him, and God wanted me to go through those in order for me to win the race. I had to endure that night.

In **Psalm 91:5–6**, God says, *"You don't have to be afraid of the dark anymore, nor fear the dangers of the day, nor dread the plagues, darkness, or disaster in the morning."*

God let me understand life, and God let me understand. God also gave me the strength and the divine energy in my trials. *My Darkest Hour* is like the book of Acts. I can never close the book without wondering what's happening next. Just like the end of a beginning, that end unleashed my life, which enabled me to do extraordinary things.

God's purpose for me was to take my brokenness, my emptiness, and my lifelessness to give me life again. It's like for me, God had all these revolving doors, and these doors were like they were designed. And he was allowing me to go in and out of these doors that he had for me. These doors were like a habitation. It was for me to transition. I had to sit back and look over my life and conclude that my end was not the end; my end was the start of a new beginning.

The moral of my story is that I've had to go through some challenges, forgiveness, trials, tribulations, testing of faith, and handling of storms to go up the mountains and make it to the hills. I have let everything go in my life for me to make it uphill. It's hard to bear a lot of sorrow. I remember it was the mountaintop, and I experienced also all the pain. I appreciate God and love him more.

I have learned so much even though it has been very slow. I may not always understand why things happen in my life as they do. I just picture Christ on the cross and everything our God has had to go through, his death and the victory over Satan. I must ask God to forgive me for complaining, even when I am at the lowest point in my life, and I just ask God to continue to strengthen me each day as I grow with him and walk with him.

If it had not been for the Lord, I would have never made it. That's why the ending of my book is the completion of my life.

When I lost my husband and my son, I was going through a storm. I used to think a storm was just doing badly; it's not. It's when you have lost a loved one, and the raining is the tears you have shed. The storm, grief, depression, emotions, losses, and wounds—all these were so heartbreaking. There was a large hole in my heart, and no one could fill that hole.

I'd been hurt, scarred, and bruised along the way. All these scarred up my memory. It was a mark on the highway. It was open, that hole in my heart. It needed to be sealed. I had to bow my head to sadness instead of keeping my head up high to heaven. I had to get a seal from God, so he could place his hands on my heart and seal and heal it.

This life journey is one of my darkest hours. I know now that God has declared my life, a life in his plans.

When I was hungry—I'm not talking about food; I mean my life—and I digested the Word, the hunger pains that I had were satisfied. I had a good life. God had my life, my plans, and God did plan it out. It was my future, and the plan was his Word. The promises he had for me were infused with the Holy Spirit.

I am aware that I have become a better and stronger woman. I know now how to react to stress and how to cope with death, pain, and suffering. I know now that the changes cannot happen until I change myself within. What is wrong in becoming loving, compassionate, and forgiving? That's just like going fishing, but instead, you're fishing for love and compassion, forgiving and learning to forgive your enemy.

I have to let everything go and, most of all, forgive; that's the key to everything. Forgiving to me has been uplifting. It's like a burden has come off my shoulder. It's been weighing me down, and when I let all that go, I've slowly started healing, and there is a new path for me. Now, when I look back, God has led me somewhere. I've learned to go sideways up the mountain. Now, since God has planned my life and put a new path for me, he must destroy everything behind me in order for me to get through the pain, long-suffering, hurt, wounds, disappointments, and all the bad experiences I've had and to find peace of mind.

This is the completion of my life, one that I've longed for. This is the story of *My Darkest Hour*. May God bless you.

About the Book

Hello. My name is Brenda Campbell, born and raised in Gladewater Texas. I have had lots of trials and tribulations throughout of my years. The book reveals the vulnerabilities of the episodes and how it knocked me down. Continuing hardships, building roadblocks and obstacles that I encountered in life. It was a battle for me, it was though all of the hardships were too much. Now that the overcoming of the struggle was an up and down battle, I took gumption for me to step up and share the story of my darkest hour. My Darkest Hour was my strength; It strengthens me and helped me move forward again. Now that I am in a good place, I can truly setback and let the world read how I survived from my Darkest Hour. It makes me feel good that I can help. As I mature, I realize that it's not just me who need help in this world.

This is my enlightened story: MY DARKEST HOUR.

www.ingramcontent.com/pod-product-compliance
Ingram Content Group UK Ltd.
Pitfield, Milton Keynes, MK11 3LW, UK
UKHW022218230426
12048UKWH00016BA/929

9 781643 673943